P9-ELW-709

Julia Child

Julia Child

An Extraordinary Life in Words and Pictures

by Erin Hagar

Art by Joanna Gorham

duopress

Copyright © 2015 by Duo Press, LLC

First Edition

Art Director: Violet Lemay
Designer: Beatriz Juarez
Editor: Robin Pinto
Copy Chief: Michele Suchomel-Casey

Hard Cover ISBN: 9781938093340
ePub ISBN: 9781938093357
Kindle ISBN: 9781938093364
PDF ISBN: 9781938093388

Library of Congress Control Number: 2014944122

For Common Core–aligned resources, please visit www.duopressbooks.com

Printed in China
1 2 3 4 5 6 7 8 9 10
duopress
www.duopressbooks.com

CONTENTS

Restaurant La Couronne
France, 1948

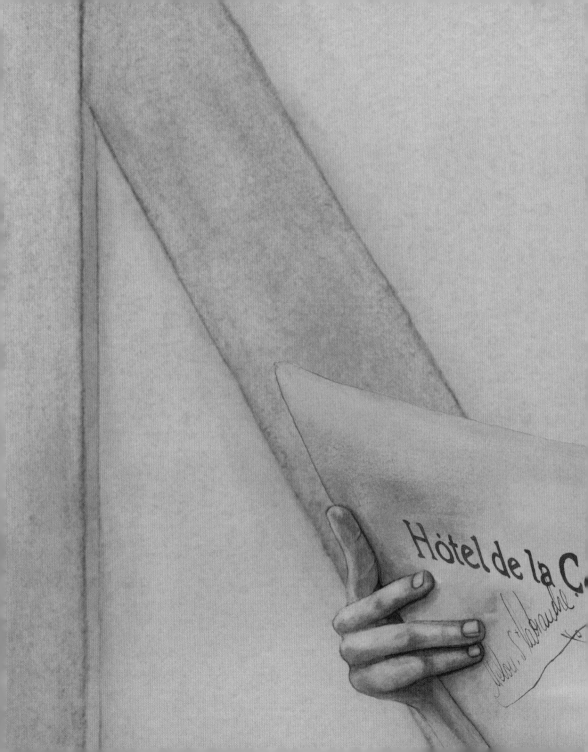

Hôtel de la C.

Hôtel de la Couronne

ROUEN

Melou, S' labaude

Menu du

MENU du L...

Hors d.Oeuv...

Sole Normande-Maison Héloise-16 Sol
Filets de Barbue Bonapar...
Maquereaux Grillé Maitreo d'
Saumon de

Ecrevisses
Homard Layonnaise Tho

Hate de Canard, Grenadile d
Lotte aux champigon...
Jambon D'York au Xér
Andouillette ou
Beurre Noisette-1
côte de Porc Grillé D

Mutton
Entrecôte ou Côtor
Pigeonn
Poulet Roti a la
ille Armoricair
ennaise

22 Aout 1932

Couvert 3

OSONS --
uniere -14+ -Trito-12
Limande Meuniere-8
-10 Morlan Colbert-8
ne-20 la Tranche
elaise ou a la Nago-2
or (prix selon grosseur)
TREES --
Oeuf Poché Bohémienne-8
Ris de Veau Clamart-16
de Mouton Rouennais -10   -10
eds
- 12 Cote de Veau Foyot -14
Chateaubriant - 16   14
mouton Pommes
Cocotte
-60a85 Sauto Ma   a95
a95 Cocotto Parme   95
-50
Lapérouse
-- LEGUMES --
Pommes Frites-5 Artichab
Haricots Vert-5
Crème-8 Choux-Flou
tan Maiso

That lunch changed everything. Those salty oysters, the buttery fish, and the light, chewy bread delighted every one of Julia Child's senses and showed her just how inspiring food could be. It was her first day in France, and Julia was thrilled to join her husband, Paul, overseas for his new job. But part of her had been wondering if she'd ever find a rewarding career of her own—something that really, truly excited her. That lunch stirred up a passion in Julia and set her on a path toward a life the thirty-six-year-old had never imagined. Years later, after her cookbooks and television shows had changed the way Americans cooked and ate, Julia would remember that lunch in Rouen, France, as "the most exciting meal of my life."

CHAPTER ONE
No Small Share of Trouble

The sun was shining, and the scent of rose bushes in bloom filled the air. A little girl, about two years old, sat alone on a curb. She was tall for her age, but she looked small against the green hills in the distance. She had wandered several blocks away from her home, but she wasn't scared or sad. Not in the least! She was having the time of her life—laughing while she threw rocks at horse-drawn buggies driving by. The game lasted until someone finally recognized her and took her home.

This girl was Julia Carolyn McWilliams, born on August 15, 1912, in sunny Pasadena, California, a town Julia would later call "paradise—just about the best place you could think of to grow up." Because the weather was beautiful all year long, Julia, her younger brother, John, and her younger sister, Dorothy (nicknamed Dort), played outside year round. They slept outside, too, on a porch that wrapped around their large house. Their father insisted on it, thinking the night air would be good for his children's lungs.

Her father, John McWilliams Jr., was a real estate developer, known for being a smart businessman and for his service to the community. Her mother, Julia Carolyn Weston McWilliams (known as Caro), was a Massachusetts girl whose family could be traced back to the earliest parts of American history—

the *Mayflower* and the Plymouth Colony. While Julia would rise to many challenges throughout her life, her wealthy family made sure she always had what she needed.

Julia's father was strict and reserved, but her mother was a warm, open person who encouraged her children's independence and freedom. Julia's grandfather John McWilliams once scolded Caro for not being tougher on young Julia for her rock-throwing and other antics. In the early 1900s, the more ladylike response would have been to respect her father-in-law's authority. But Caro stood firm. "She's a child, for goodness sake," she replied, refusing to punish Julia.

Caro was used to challenging the idea of what women should do. In an era when most women married right after high school, Caro graduated from Smith College, a prestigious all-women's Ivy League school. She didn't marry until she was thirty-three, and she parented her children with a light touch, giving them the freedom to explore and play.

This suited Julia just fine. From an early age, she was the center of the action, the life of the party, the ringleader for all kinds of adventures and mayhem. Her mother wrote in her diary that Julia was "always the instigator," and she worried that Julia's curiosity would make it hard to keep track of her. "One of these days we'll have to put up a fence," her mother would say. And she was right. As soon as she could, Julia took off on her tricycle around the block, racing right along with the horse-drawn buggies and trolley cars, ready to go where her curiosity led her.

When she got a little older and the tricycle turned into a bicycle,

Julia and her best friend, Babe Hall, would cruise the neighborhood together, baskets filled with the ingredients for adventure—scissors, thread, matches, nails, and anything they could grab that might come in handy. If Julia and Babe had written a book about their childhood, they might have called it *What Would Happen If . . . ?* What would happen if they made mud pies and flung them at cars from the roof of the garage? (An angry driver would climb the roof and threaten to take the girls to the police.) What would happen if they climbed a gutter to explore the inside of a vacant house? (Julia would catch her finger on a wire and dangle in midair until jumping down, leaving a chunk of skin behind her.) What would happen if they stole cigarettes and cigars and smoked them up high in an oak tree? (Julia's father would find them and offer Julia a $1,000 savings bond if she swore not to smoke until she was twenty-one. Julia kept her promise, took the money, and then smoked every day for the next thirty years.) Julia's curiosity led them to a whole lot of fun, and no small share of trouble.

Trouble didn't worry Julia, not if it meant she got what she wanted. When her father insisted that the family dog stay home during their summer vacation, Julia campaigned to bring him along. Arguing didn't change her father's mind, so Julia hid the dog in a laundry basket in the back of the car until the family had traveled too far to turn back. Then she let the dog out. Surprise!

Julia was a natural prankster. Her siblings made easy targets, especially Dort, who was five years younger. When Dort was ready to come inside after playing, Julia would lock the front door. When she finally let Dort in, Julia would pretend not to recognize her.

"Who are you? What do you want here?" she'd ask. Pretending her sister was an intruder, Julia would threaten to call the police.

All that activity was enough to make a girl hungry, and, boy, could Julia eat! "I had the appetite of a wolf," she said, a trait that continued into her adulthood. It wasn't just her activity that brought out her appetite. Julia took the phrase "growing girl" to new heights—literally! She was at least a head taller than anyone else her age and "one size bigger than you could ever buy," she remembered.

Hungry as she was, Julia didn't give a whit how food was made. "As a girl, I had zero interest in the stove," she wrote in her autobiography. Mostly Julia thought the kitchen was "dismal."

Julia's mother spent as little time in the kitchen as possible, much preferring to play tennis and visit her friends. Like many wealthy Pasadena families, Julia's family employed a cook, who'd prepare basic meat and potatoes, maybe a roast leg of lamb for Sunday dinners with Julia's grandparents, who lived nearby. When the cook had a night off, Julia's mother made one of her three recipes: herbed biscuits, Welsh rarebit (a thick, cheesy sauce served over toast), or fried codfish balls, a throwback to her New England roots. The food filled them up, but it wasn't anything special.

There was one person whose cooking made a strong impression on young Julia. "Grandmother McWilliams was a great cook who made wonderful donuts and the best broiled chicken I ever ate," Julia said. Her grandmother would set those donuts—deep-fried cake batter, dusted in powdered sugar, with a hint of nutmeg—on the kitchen windowsill to cool, attracting Julia like a moth to a flame.

CHAPTER TWO
"An Adolescent Nut"

In 1927, when Julia was fifteen, she left home to attend the Katharine Branson School. Boarding school was a tradition in her mother's family, and Julia's parents thought that it would smooth out Julia's rough edges, calm her down a bit, and channel her confidence and leadership skills toward more productive activities.

The Katharine Branson School was an all-girls school in Northern California, about 400 miles from Pasadena. The campus felt like an overnight summer camp, its Mission-style buildings surrounded by woods and mountains. The girls spent as much time on athletics and outdoor activities, which Julia loved, as they did on academics, which she didn't. Because women were expected to marry and have children instead of pursuing careers, many high schools in 1927 taught domestic tasks like cooking and sewing to their female students. But girls at the Katharine Branson School were not training to be housewives; they were preparing for college. The academic program was serious, even if Julia didn't treat it that way.

Julia spent more time showing her school spirit than studying for her classes. She participated in all kinds of activities—student government, the basketball team, even a hiking club. Julia's height—she would grow to six feet, two inches—meant that when the school play rolled around, she was "usually cast as a fish

25

or something. Never as the beautiful princess." She liked almost everything about life at the school, even the crummy meals, with one exception: being forced to attend church every week. One Sunday, in protest, she convinced all her classmates to wear their uniform hats backward to the service. "We thought it was terribly funny," she remembered later, "but no one noticed."

What Julia's fellow KBS students remembered most about Julia was her personality. One of her friends said that Julia "[felt] at home and at ease anywhere." It was, the friend continued, "the secret to her charm and appeal." At her graduation ceremony in 1930, Julia received the First Citizen Award for her spirit and service to the school.

After high school, Julia followed her mother's footsteps across the country to Smith College, the all-women's college in Northampton, Massachusetts. Julia would joke later that she was "enrolled at Smith College at birth." But the transition from high school to college wasn't easy.

Julia's first weeks at Smith were one of the few times in her life when she felt she didn't fit in. For one thing, her bed was too short for her six-foot-two body—she literally didn't fit! (A phone call to the facilities office quickly changed that.) Her clothes presented another challenge. Julia was a tall, gangly girl from the West Coast on a campus full of Easterners with a distinct style: pastel tweed skirts, crew neck sweaters, brown and white Spaulding saddle shoes, and a strand of imitation pearls. In her gingham and lace, Julia stood out like a sore thumb.

She was miserable until Thanksgiving, when her mother came from California and took her shopping in New York City.

But despite small bumps in the road, Julia took to Smith in her usual Julia way. She became fast friends with her roommate, Mary Case, even though Mary was quite studious. Once, they played a prank on faculty resident Dr. Abbie O'Keefe, who lived directly below the girls. While Dr. O'Keefe was having other faculty members over for tea, Julia and Mary lowered a rug out of their window, making Dr. O'Keefe's residence as dark as night. The girls would break out into giggles so often that poor Mary would hang a bedspread in the middle of the room in an attempt to block her view of Julia while she studied. Julia would throw jelly donuts—one of her favorite foods—over the bedspread to distract Mary. "I was an adolescent nut," Julia would later say about her time at Smith.

"Someone like me should not have been accepted at a serious institution."

Julia majored in history and studied French. She thought she might be a "lady novelist," though she didn't take any writing courses. "I spent my time growing up and doing just enough work to get by," she said. Sure, she was having a good time, but it was difficult for Julia to look ahead to her future. "When I went [to Smith] in the '30's," she said, "women had no careers. You could be a mother or maybe a nurse or a secretary. But you couldn't be a lawyer or a banker. . . . We were just sort of drifting around." Julia didn't want to be a nurse or a secretary—she didn't know what she wanted to be. After graduation in 1934, she went back home to California.

Without a job, Julia kept herself busy by having fun. She threw big parties at her family's home and at their beach house, and she went to parties thrown by her friends. But she was restless. She wanted to do something that engaged her. Julia thought she wanted a "literary" career, maybe in newspapers or magazines. She couldn't find anything. When her sister moved to the East Coast to attend college, Julia's parents made arrangements for her to go, too. She'd live with an aunt in Massachusetts while she attended secretarial school and applied for jobs. Before long, Julia was offered a position at the W. & J. Sloane furniture company in New York City. She got an aparment with a few Smith classmates and started work, writing product descriptions for newspaper advertisements and doing some secretarial tasks. At least she could write a little. Maybe, she thought, this experience would put her one step closer to her goal of being a lady novelist.

Julia enjoyed the bustle of the city, eating lunch at coffee shops when she could afford it, attending parties and plays, and submitting her writing to magazines like the *New Yorker* and having it rejected. While she wasn't thrilled with her job, one area of her life had improved—she finally had a boyfriend. His name was Tom Johnston, and Julia adored him. She wrote in her diary that she had "never been profoundly in love before." But Tom broke Julia's heart, marrying one of her classmates. This heartbreak, combined with her boredom at work, nudged Julia back to California in the spring of 1937.

Two months after she returned to Pasadena, Julia experienced a heartbreak of a different kind. Her mother, only sixty years old, died after struggling with severe high blood pressure for many years. Julia had known her mother wasn't well, but no one knew how ill she really was. After a small service at their family home, Julia's brother and sister went back to the East Coast, while Julia stayed behind with her father.

Her mother's death rattled Julia, pushing her into one of the darkest moments in her life. Anyone watching Julia from the outside would see a typical society woman flitting around like a butterfly from thing to thing—golf and tennis at the club, parties and weddings, civic activities and volunteer work. But deep down, she was miserable, aching to do something more. "I shall be interested to see if I am ever a happy success," she wrote in her diary during this time.

Julia still missed her mother terribly, but the heartache from losing Tom slowly faded. After spending some time reflecting about her life, Julia decided that she wasn't going to worry about being alone. "I am quite content to be the way I am—and feel quite superior to many a wedded mouse. By god—I can do what I want!" she wrote in her diary. Her confidence got another boost when she took a job at the Beverly Hills branch of the W. & J. Sloane furniture company, the same company she'd worked for in New York. This time, she was in charge of public relations and advertising. The job didn't last long, however. She was fired after not completing a task her bosses asked her to do.

Julia didn't let it get her down too much. She had learned a lot about managing an office, skills that might be useful someday. If she could only figure out what kind of career she actually wanted…

CHAPTER THREE
Too Tall for the Navy

In the summer of 1940, when Julia was twenty-eight years old, she had the opportunity to become a "wedded mouse" herself. Harrison Chandler was, like Julia, a wealthy Pasadenan who ran in the same social circles as the McWilliams family. The Chandlers owned the newspaper the *Los Angeles Times*, and Julia's father very much approved of the match. Julia was surprised by the proposal, but she wasn't sure. Marrying Harrison would answer the big question about what to do with her future. She wouldn't need to choose a career because, at that time, most married women didn't work. It would have been easy, but she wasn't in love.

Julia said no.

To pass the time, Julia volunteered for the Pasadena Red Cross, performing office work for the emergency response organization. And then world events set her on a different path. Like most of the country, Julia was shocked into action when the Japanese conducted a surprise attack on the U.S. Naval base at Pearl Harbor, Hawaii, on December 7, 1941. Until that moment, most Americans didn't want to get involved in World War II, but the attack—which killed almost 2,500 U.S. citizens—changed everything. The next day, President Franklin Roosevelt declared war on Japan, and three days later the United States was officially at war with

Japan and its allies, Germany and Italy.

Civilian groups sprang up to help however they could. Julia spent hours in a windowless room in Los Angeles, receiving radio reports of shipping vessels along the coast. She would mark their locations on a map (much like the game Battleship), and military staff would transmit relevant information to their units in the field.

It was useful work. The entire western coastline of the United States was unguarded, and Japanese vessels had been spotted very close to places like Santa Barbara, California. Still, Julia wanted more. More action, more adventure, more space between her and Harrison Chandler. She applied to the women's auxiliary unit of the U.S. Navy, took the civil service exam, and moved back across the country to Washington, D.C. She was thirty years old.

Emerging from the train station for the first time in D.C., Julia saw the U.S. Capitol building framing the summer sky and blocky federal buildings all around. There were loads of people moving about—people busy doing real work, patriotic work. Julia loved the energy of this place. It was exhilarating!

She settled in and quickly learned that the Naval Reserve had rejected her—an "automatic disqualification" on physical grounds. Julia was healthy as a horse, so what could possibly be the reason? Then she saw her application. Someone had circled the space on the form where she'd recorded her height.

Julia McWilliams was too tall for the navy!

No matter. Julia wanted to help the war effort, so she applied for office work all over the city. Eventually she landed a job in the

Office of War Information, where she typed up index cards with the names of every government official found in newspaper articles and government documents. After two months and 10,000 cards, that was enough of that.

In 1942, almost exactly one year after the attack on Pearl Harbor, Julia began working for the Office of Strategic Services (OSS)—America's first intelligence gathering agency. The OSS, which would later become today's Central Intelligence Agency (CIA), coordinated the missions of American spies working in enemy territories. Julia strode into the OSS building on her first day, fabulously confident in a new leopard-print coat, thrilled to be part of this new opportunity. Even though she was still typing and filing, Julia loved the idea of working in intelligence. She worked hard, six days a week. Her supervisors noticed her efforts and gave her more responsibility. She even became a supervisor herself, managing eight other people.

Julia downplayed her contribution, calling her responsibilities "just office work." But in a spy unit, information is like gold, and Julia had her hands on lots of it. She had one of the highest levels of security clearance a civilian could have. She knew the agents' code names, as well as their locations and missions. She processed maps, so she knew the locations of the enemy supply routes, munitions dumps, and industrial facilities. One operative called Julia the "keeper of the secrets."

Julia worked for a bit in the division that tested survival equipment—things like shark repellent and exposure suits—for pilots who'd been shot down over the ocean. One day, Julia was asked to go to the market to buy some fish. Researchers wanted to know if a soldier lost at sea could survive by squeezing fish juice into his mouth. She told people later that she worked for the "fish-squeezing unit" of the OSS.

After three years in Washington, despite receiving a few promotions, Julia felt stuck. "I didn't have any languages," she said later. "I naturally wasn't trained as a spy. My history background didn't amount to anything." She didn't expect to be offered more interesting opportunities if she stayed in Washington. But the OSS was opening bases overseas, as the war in Asia became more complicated. It needed administrative personnel, like Julia, to support the spy operations against Japan. Working overseas might be just the boost her career—and her adventurous spirit—needed. When offered the opportunity to be transferred to the South East Asia Command in India, Julia jumped at the chance.

CHAPTER FOUR
Julia in the World

In February of 1944, thirty-two-year-old Julia boarded a train full of soldiers—one of only three women on the entire train—and traveled from Washington to California, the first leg of her new adventure. She had a few weeks of training, where she was issued a uniform and a gas mask and learned some survival skills—how to evacuate a ship by sliding down a rope over the side, for example. Then she boarded the SS *Mariposa*, one of nine women among 3,000 men, and made her way to the war in the East.

Julia loved meeting the smart people headed to India with her—men and women trained as anthropologists, journalists, artists, photographers, and missionaries. Despite having attended one of the best colleges in the country, Julia considered her time with the OSS her "first real encounter with the academic mind." In a letter to a friend years later, she wrote, "I found, suddenly, that these professional people were what I'd been missing all my life." Her conversations with her fellow shipmates were deep and filled with big ideas that Julia didn't always understand. Still, she soaked them up like rays of California sunshine. On that ship, eating navy food around a table with these fascinating people, Julia resolved to pay more attention to the life of her mind.

Until her ship docked in Bombay, India, Julia had been out of the United States only once: a family trip to Tijuana, Mexico, just over the California border. The highlight of that trip had been eating the newly invented Caesar salad. In Bombay, Julia's senses tingled as she disembarked the ship—smelling the incense and cigarettes, hearing the horses' hooves *clip-clop* as they pulled carriages loaded with passengers. "Have met practically no one who likes India," she wrote in her diary. "I *do*!"

Julia toured as much of Bombay as she could and went golfing and dancing. In her diary, she wrote about the markets, describing fruit and vegetable baskets with live chickens resting on them, and how the children would swarm around her and laugh (probably at her height). Then, after eighteen days in India, Julia learned that the headquarters of the South East Asia Command would be moved to Kandy, Ceylon (now Sri Lanka), an island nation south of India.

After a hot and dusty train ride to Madras (now Chennai), India, then a ferry ride through the Bay of Bengal, Julia arrived in Ceylon on April 25, 1944, to start her job as head of the Registry. She would be in charge of organizing all the classified papers for the command. It was, one of her colleagues noted later, "a truly awesome responsibility," one that required a level of seriousness Julia hadn't known she had before working in Washington.

Her work was important, but boring. Julia entertained herself by playing pranks on her coworkers. Once, she wrote a joking memo to a colleague back in the States, threatening to send a pouch filled with "itching powder and various bacteriological diseases" if she didn't get a report she needed soon.

At least the location was lovely. Kandy, Ceylon, was considered one of the most beautiful places in the world. There were coconut palms and papaya trees, tranquil rice paddies, and Buddhist temples in the foothills. The OSS headquarters was set on a tea plantation, lush and green. Monkeys played in the trees above. Julia called the air "skin-warm," perfect to the touch. The staff worked in palm-thatched huts known as *bashas*, and there was a dining area and a social club. Cobras and scorpions might have kept some from calling the headquarters "luxurious," but it was pretty darn close.

In Kandy, far away from battles and bloodshed, the OSS staff could enjoy themselves at the end of the workday. There were cocktail hours and parties and movies on the base. Romance bloomed between some OSS employees, but not for Julia. Instead, she enjoyed picnics with small groups of friends and trips to visit local sites like Buddhist cave temples.

One of the men who joined Julia and others on these outings was Paul Child. A talented artist, Paul worked for the Visual Presentation branch of the OSS. In an era before computers and satellites, creative types like Paul added their skills to the war effort by making maps, charts, and diagrams. He had been transferred to Ceylon to design the war room for Lord Mountbatten, the Supreme Allied Commander in Southeast Asia.

A painter and photographer, a musician, a lover of food and wine and big ideas, Paul spoke fluent French, played the violin, and was a black belt in Judo. He was ten years older than Julia, and he was lonely. His long-time partner, Edith Kennedy, had died a few years earlier, which devastated him. Now, in Ceylon, Paul was looking for love.

But he wasn't interested in a romance with Julia McWilliams. Paul wrote to his twin brother, Charlie, that Julia had a "slight atmosphere of hysteria" that bothered him. He noted that she gasped when she talked, especially when she got excited. Part of what Paul noticed must have had to do with Julia's unique voice. That voice! It warbled like an exotic bird, climbing and dipping like notes on a music scale, occasionally wheezy or breathless. Her voice was something she inherited from her mother's family; the Westons called it "hooting." Some think it was a result of stretched vocal chords, which would make sense. Everything about the six-foot-two Julia was long and stretched. Whatever its cause, Paul certainly didn't find it—or much else about Julia—attractive.

To be fair, the feeling was mutual. Julia noted in her diary that Paul was too old, too short, too bald, with an "unbecoming blond moustache and a long, unbecoming nose." But he was also smart, cultured, and artistic. Julia loved listening to him talk, the way he wove his knowledge and experiences into dizzying conversations.

One Sunday, Julia took a trip with Paul to see something extraordinary.

Kandy, Ceylon
1944

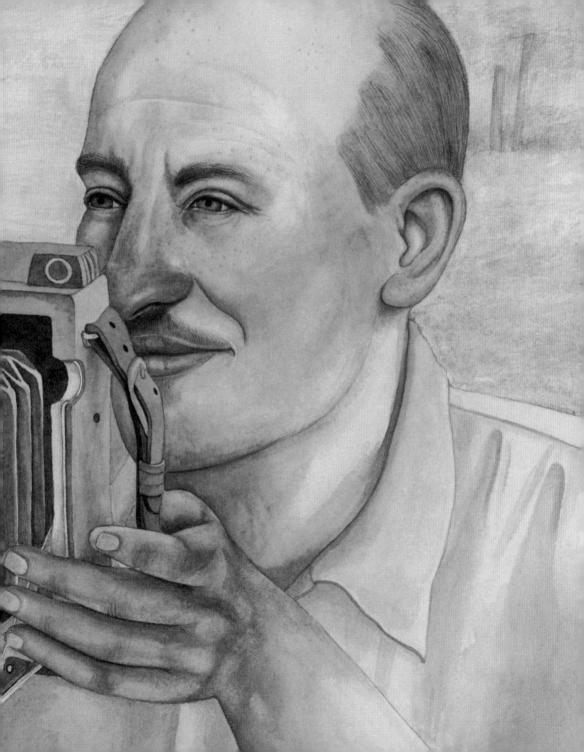

John McWilliams
25 Magnolia Avenue
Pasadena, California

CEYLON
15 CENTS

CHAPTER FIVE
"Dearest One"

By the end of that lovely afternoon, Julia had a change of heart. "Wish I were in love," she wrote that night in her diary. "And that what I considered *really attractive* was in love with me."

Paul might not have considered himself in love yet, but his feelings toward Julia were slowly changing. One of his letters to his twin brother, Charlie, showed a softening toward her, if not attraction yet. "She has a somewhat ragged, but pleasantly crazy sense of humor." A bit later, Paul wrote that Julia was "warm and witty" and "*extremely* likable and pleasant to be around." He could sense Julia's feelings for him.

But it wouldn't matter anyway, Paul thought. He knew he would soon be transferred from Kandy to Chongqing, China. When the day of his transfer arrived, in January of 1945, it took them both by surprise. Paul left Ceylon with two hours' notice, and Julia hardly had time to say good-bye. Julia was depressed after he left; any spark between them would be snuffed by the distance. Who knew if they'd even see each other again?

Not only was Julia depressed about Paul, but she was bored with her work. Maybe a change of scenery would be good, she thought. Julia asked for a transfer. She, too, was sent to China, but to Kunming, 400 miles away from where Paul was stationed.

To get to her new post, Julia had to fly "the Hump," from Calcutta, India, to Kunming, China, over the peaks of the Himalayan Mountains. It was the deadliest air route of the war, nicknamed the "aluminum trail" because the air currents at that altitude could break planes apart. Hundreds of planes had crashed making the same journey. During Julia's flight, the plane suddenly began to lose altitude, plummeting downward. The lights went out. Some of the passengers threw up. Julia sat reading a book throughout the treacherous flight, cool as a cucumber, as if she barely noticed anything unusual.

The war felt closer in China. There was a sense of urgency and tension that Julia hadn't felt at her previous post. She organized secret papers, invented a simpler system for the code names the OSS used, and managed the payments distributed to local spies. Still, she was bored, and she missed the carefree social life in Ceylon. She missed Paul.

Until April, that is, when he was transferred to Kunming.

In Kunming, Paul and Julia's relationship took a turn. They spent more time together, by themselves. Their favorite moments would, as they would in the future, center around food. They both found the meals on the base to be "terrible army food," as Julia would call it. But "the Chinese food was wonderful. We ate out as often as we could."

Paul searched for the best, most authentic restaurants. He taught Julia to use chopsticks and introduced her to new kinds of food. One of their favorites was rice noodles in thick stock served with thin raw chicken that would cook immediately when hot broth was poured over it. There was fish in plantain leaves, duck with bamboo fungus. Julia loved the flavors and the spices, the combinations of tastes, the way the Chinese made these "great swooping, slurping noises as they ate." She also loved talking about food with Paul. He told her stories about his time living in France and described his favorite foods from that country. Good cooking, Julia discovered, made for fascinating conversations.

Of course, she and Paul talked about other things, too. Over tables piled high with dishes, they told each other about their families, past relationships, and former careers. They wondered about the future, what they'd do when the war was over. Neither of them had a job to go back to in America.

When the war ended in 1945, Julia went home to California, and Paul took a job in Washington, D.C. They made plans for Paul to visit in the summer of 1946, and while she waited Julia took cooking classes. If food and cooking were that important to Paul, by gosh, she'd have to get better at it. Her efforts frequently ended in disaster, like the time a duck exploded in the oven because she forgot to pierce the skin before cooking it. She shared these experiences in letters to Paul. Paul wrote back, encouraging her efforts. He said he had no doubt she'd eventually be a "wonderful cook because you are so interested in food." Little did he know how much he had to do with that interest! Over time, their letters became more and more romantic, seasoned with phrases like "dearest one" and "I adore you."

Finally, in July of 1946, Paul and Julia were reunited. Paul took the train from Washington, D.C., to Pasadena to meet Julia's family. Then the two of them drove back across the country, ending up at Paul's brother's cabin in Maine, where Julia met his family. The trip was so splendid, and the two were so compatible, that they made plans to marry on September 1.

While running some pre-wedding errands, Paul and Julia suffered a serious car accident—Julia was tossed out of the vehicle! Did they let that slow them down?

Not a chance.

Paul walked down the aisle with a cane; Julia had a bandage above her left eye, and the pictures show a couple that couldn't be happier. Julia was thirty-four years old and married to the smartest, most interesting man she'd ever met.

Right after the wedding, Mr. and Mrs. Paul Child moved to Washington, D.C. Paul had a job with the State Department, and Julia, for the moment, was a happy homemaker. She decorated their house on Wisconsin Avenue, hanging some of Paul's best photographs along the staircase and organizing her collection of cookbooks on a shelf in the kitchen. But using those cookbooks to make anything decent to eat? Well, that was a challenge.

"I was hopeless," Julia would later say about her early cooking attempts. "Nothing I did seemed right. The kitchen was a place I truly enjoyed being, but I was convinced I had no talent for making food that tasted good." Her cooking lessons hadn't scratched the surface of what Julia needed to know. She tried to broil a chicken but managed to burn it after twenty minutes. ("I needed better directions," she said.) She invited a college friend over for codfish chowder, but it turned into codfish mush instead. One night, thinking Paul would appreciate something fancy, Julia tried a recipe for beef heart. The results of that little experiment ended up *immediately* in the garbage can. It took her so long to get a meal together that often she and Paul wouldn't eat until 10 p.m.

But Julia was not one to give up. Paul's brother Charlie lived a few blocks away, and his wife, Freddie, was great cook. Julia took informal cooking lessons from Freddie, learning the basics while enjoying their friendship. Freddie showed Julia that good cooks make mistakes, too—they just know how to fix them. As many mistakes as Julia made, this was an important lesson.

Julia and Paul entertained often, giving her many opportunities to practice cooking. They loved having a home in Washington, near so many interesting people—OSS colleagues and artists and policy makers, intellectuals of every type. "Paul loved brilliant talk," Julia said. And the two made a good team. Julia didn't pay much attention to the little details, but Paul set a perfect table and made sure everyone's wine glass was full. Paul wasn't very outgoing, but Julia made everyone feel warm and welcome. The dinners may not have tasted very good, but the conversations were something to feast on.

One night, after a quiet evening making Valentine's Day cards for family and friends—an annual tradition— Julia and Paul awoke to the acidic smell of smoke. FIRE! They spent a frantic few minutes tossing any bits of clothing they could grab out the window. Julia focused on saving her shoes—always difficult to find in her size. As smoke and heat filled their bedroom, they crawled to the living room, where they could climb out the window. They landed safely on the sidewalk below, wearing only thin bathrobes in the freezing February night.

The fire, which had started in the house next door, destroyed their home. Julia and Paul were lucky to make it out alive, and lucky, too, that Charlie and Freddie lived close by. They moved in with them while repairs were made. To make things worse, Paul learned that he had lost his job with the State Department. Julia tried her best to lighten the mood, but it was a dark time, especially for Paul.

After a few months, things started looking up. Julia and Paul found a new house, they took a long summer vacation in Maine, and Paul got a new job with the State Department, one that would use more of his artistic skills and would move them overseas. But where? They hadn't the foggiest idea where they'd be stationed, but they were excited for the chance at adventure. It could be India, given their experience with the OSS. It might be Germany or Belgium. When the word finally came, neither could believe their luck—Julia and Paul were headed to Paris, France!

Paris!

Paul had lived there years before, and it was his favorite place in the world. Now he could show Julia everything he loved about it. It would be an education unlike anything she'd experienced. In a matter of months, Paul and Julia had rented out their house, boxed up the things they'd leave behind, and found a new home for their cat. They arranged to have their Buick station wagon, nicknamed the "Blue Flash," shipped over with them. In October of 1948, they boarded the SS *America* out of New York City and set sail.

CHAPTER SIX
"You Do Like to Eat"

After five days on stormy seas, Julia stumbled toward the porthole for her first view of France. Rain speckled the window and the sun wasn't up, so she didn't see much—just a few lights twinkling in the distance and the grey outline of the horizon. Julia didn't know what to expect from France, and this view certainly wasn't helping.

Once the ship had docked and their belongings were unloaded, they drove toward Paris. Along the way, they stopped to have lunch at a restaurant named La Couronne in the little town of Rouen. That was the lunch—the salty oysters and buttery fish—that changed the course of Julia's life forever.

Julia watched the French countryside out the passenger window as the afternoon wore on. The shadowy light of dusk settled around the Blue Flash, and the silhouette of the Eiffel Tower emerged on the horizon, outlined in blinking red lights. They had arrived.

Paul and Julia settled into a hotel and ate a dinner that was "fine," Julia remembered, "but nothing compared to La Couronne." Then they got on with the business of starting their lives in France.

Paul managed an office that designed and promoted exhibits of American visual material (art, photographs, and other displays) to the French. The goal of these exhibits was to foster a good relationship between the two countries. Julia's job, for the moment, was to run errands that would get them settled in—basic things like taking the car to the mechanic, buying slippers, leaving business cards at the homes of the fellow State Department employees to introduce themselves—things most people don't have to think twice about. But in a new place, in a foreign language, even ordinary tasks are filled with a sense of adventure. At least, that was how Julia approached it.

On their first Saturday in Paris, the sun twinkled in a bright blue sky—a perfect invitation to tour the city on foot. It became a habit that Julia and Paul would continue almost every weekend they lived there. They lingered over interesting architecture, strolled through parks, explored places Paul remembered, like the Deux Magots café, Paul's favorite from his stay twenty years earlier, and the American church where he'd helped install the stained glass windows.

The war had taken its toll on the city and its people. The Germans had bombed Paris, so some of the buildings Paul remembered were either gone or reduced to piles of rubble. But even with all the reminders of those difficult times, there was just something about Paris. Julia walked around, open-mouthed at the beauty, the history of it all. She loved walking along the Seine River and seeing the ancient churches, and famous museums. Everything about the city struck a chord in her.

Julia and Paul tried all kinds of restaurants—comfortable bistros with cats sleeping on the chairs, fancy restaurants with celebrities tucked away from view, and everything in between. The first few times they ate out, Julia ordered the same fish—*sole muniere*—she'd loved so much at La Couronne. She couldn't imagine that anything else could be as delicious! It didn't take her long to figure out that there were dozens, hundreds, of delicious things to try. Steamed mussels and braised kidneys, pears grown right in the city, and all kinds of cheeses. She loved it all. "Julie wants to spend the rest of her life right here, eating sole, . . . drinking wine and looking at Paris," Paul wrote to his brother.

The only thing missing was Julia's ability to speak French. She'd studied the language a bit in school, though her accent had made her teachers cringe. "My French 'u's were only worse than my 'o's," Julia said. She muddled through during those early days in Paris, but as time wore on, she got more and more upset. "I am a talker, and my inability to communicate was hugely frustrating," she remembered. The breaking point came at a Thanksgiving party. Julia loved parties—she loved people! But over half of the guests at this party were French, and Julia struggled to keep up interesting conversations with any of them. "I've had it!" she told Paul later that night. "I'm going to learn to speak this language, come hell or high water."

A few days later, Julia enrolled in French classes—two hours a day, three times a week. Paul helped her at home. But, social creature that she was, Julia's best French instruction came from her new friend, Hélène Baltrusaitis. She and Julia would meet in cafés and restaurants. Hélène would work with Julia on her French, and Julia would help Hélène with her English. It was Hélène who loaned Julia her first French cookbook, written by the famous chef Ali-Bab. Julia poured over the "succulent" recipes. She loved the way a chef could make a cookbook funny, and she read it every night before bed "with the passionate devotion of a fourteen-year-old boy to True Detective stories," Paul joked.

As much as Julia loved touring Paris and learning French, she and Paul both knew she needed something more. She refused to go back to office work. It had bored her in D.C., Ceylon, and China, and she certainly didn't want to spend her time in Paris stuck inside a stuffy office. She grasped at anything, even enrolling in a hat-making course to pass the time. "Awful, awful," she recalled.

They both wanted her to find something fulfilling, something she loved. What else could she do?

"You do like to eat, Julia," Paul reminded her.

Yes, she did like to eat. She'd been cooking more, too. As her French improved, Julia spent more and more time at her local market, getting to know the shopkeepers and learning about all kinds of foods, like snails and shallots and new types of cheeses. The shopkeepers taught her how to choose the best items and gave her cooking tips. Julia experimented with new recipes and cooking techniques at home, using the famous 1,087-page French cookbook *Larousse Gastronomique* that Paul had bought her for her thirty-seventh birthday.

But something was missing, she thought. "I wanted to roll up my sleeves and dive into French cuisine," Julia remembered later. "But how?" French cooking was known for being complex and difficult to learn.

On a June day in 1949, Julia visited Paris's most famous cooking school, Le Cordon Bleu, where serious cooking students are trained by some of the best chefs in the world. The school was just another gray building on a street full of gray buildings. It would have been easy to miss. But for one of the first times in her life, Julia knew exactly what she was looking for. Julia watched a demonstration lesson and "was hooked." She signed herself up to start in October, barreling her way into a year-long course on advanced French cuisine for professional restaurateurs. She couldn't have been more excited.

Le Cordon Bleu
Paris, France
1949

CHAPTER SEVEN
"Such Fun!"

Julia's class was filled with about a dozen former American soldiers taking advantage of a government tuition program. Walking into the class for the first time, Julia got the sense she was invading their "boy's club." No matter. "I had spent most of the war in male-dominated environments," Julia wrote. "[I] wasn't fazed by them in the least."

The class met in the hot and crowded basement kitchen of Le Cordon Bleu. The school was having financial problems, and it showed. The students in Julia's class had only the basics—an icebox instead of an electric refrigerator, a few stoves, some small electric ovens. Certainly nothing fancy like the new electric blenders or mixers that were just becoming available.

None of this bothered Julia, who quickly settled in and got to work. She adored her instructor, Chef Max Bugnard, a kind and gentle man in his seventies who'd spent his life cooking. Chef Bugnard was a good teacher, but he moved through lots of information quickly. His "rat-a-tat" delivery was hard to follow, and Julia was glad she'd taken French classes. "[T]he Cordon Bleu was a lesson in language as well as cookery," she later said. She asked a lot of questions, never afraid to look dumb in front her classmates. "I was never the only one confused," Julia wrote.

Chef Bugnard focused on the fundamentals. He taught his students how to properly slice onions for soup and how to give potatoes and carrot chunks a seven-sided cut so they'd cook evenly in stews. Julia learned how to defeather, clean, and debone a chicken. They worked their way through the sauces for meats, fish, and vegetables.

One day during her first week, Julia learned that even simple things had to be done the "right" way. Chef Bugnard invited a student to make scrambled eggs in front the class. When none of the men volunteered, Julia made her way to the stove, slapped some butter in a hot pan, and whipped up some eggs with cream.

Chef Bugnard was horrified. "*Non!* That is absolutely wrong!" He showed the class how to gently blend the yolks and whites, how to keep the heat low and let the eggs cook slowly—almost three full minutes—before taking them off the burner, stirring them with a fork, and adding the cream. It was a "remarkable lesson" for Julia, not so much because of how the eggs tasted, but because of the time and attention Chef Bugnard gave to such an ordinary dish. "You never forget a beautiful thing that you have made," he told them. Julia learned a lot from Chef Bugnard, but this idea—that every dish deserves a cook's best effort—was perhaps the most important thing he taught her.

Almost immediately, Julia fell into a routine that kept her bustling from morning to night. She'd wake every morning by 6:30, grab a croissant and coffee at her favorite café, then head to Le Cordon Bleu to peel onions or do other prep work for her class with Chef Bugnard, which started at 7:30. When class ended two hours later, Julia would race to her favorite open-air Parisian market, where she'd buy all the ingredients they'd used that morning. At home, she'd do her best to re-create her morning's lesson for Paul, who'd come home from his job at the embassy for lunch. After lunch and a quick rest, Julia would head back to Le Cordon Bleu for the afternoon's demonstration lesson.

Julia loved the demonstration lessons. They took place in a room that resembled a small auditorium, with students watching a visiting chef and his assistants as they prepared complex dishes on a well-lit kitchen stage. It was like watching a play of cooking, except that students could call out questions as the chefs worked. Julia would take lots of notes, then race home to put what she'd seen into practice for dinner.

"If you could see Julie stuffing pepper and lard up the [butt] hole of a dead pigeon, you'd realize how profoundly affected she's been already by the Cordon Bleu," Paul wrote to his brother during Julia's first week at the school. It was true. Julia had finally found her passion and had jumped in with both feet. That first week alone, she prepared a stuffed pigeon, a beef stew, and a dish with veal and beans. "I had never taken anything so seriously in my life—husband and cat excepted—and I could hardly bear to be away from the kitchen," she wrote in her memoir years later. "What fun! What a revelation! . . . How magnificent to find my life's calling at long last!"

Paul never wavered in his support of Julia and her cooking. Their tiny kitchen overflowed with every kind of cooking gadget.

One Sunday Paul lugged an enormous mortar and pestle through a Parisian flea market for Julia so she could use it to pound fish into little creamy bites of *quenelles de brochet*. Paul jokingly referred to himself as a "Cordon Bleu widower" because he almost never saw Julia unless he watched her cook. But he was thrilled about her success. "Julie's cookery is actually improving!" he wrote his family. "I didn't quite believe it would, just between us girls, but it really is. ...I envy her this chance. It would be such fun doing it at the same time with her." And lucky for Paul, he got to eat all the delicious things she was making, even if all that rich butter and cream sometimes gave him a stomach ache.

One day, after a couple of months at Le Cordon Bleu, Julia invited her friend Winnie over for lunch. Perhaps Julia had gotten a little too confident in her cooking. She decided she didn't need to measure the flour for the *sauce Mornay*. (It came out thick and gloppy.) She also decided that chicory—a bitter, leafy green— would be an acceptable substitute for spinach. (It wasn't.) Julia called the lunch she served poor Winnie "the most vile eggs Florentine one could imagine." Did Julia apologize and make excuses for her terrible meal? Of course not! Things go wrong in the kitchen sometimes—that's life. There was no point making the lunch any worse than it was by drawing attention to it. "Never apologize" became one of Julia's famous sayings. "[I]f the food is truly vile, as my ... eggs Florentine surely were, then the cook must simply grit her teeth and bear it with a smile—and learn from her mistakes."

In January of 1950, when her class started up again

after the holiday break, Julia realized that she had been cooking nonstop for two months, but she had barely scratched the surface of all she wanted to know. "[T]he more I learned," she wrote, "the more I realized how very much one has to know before one is in-the-know at all." It wasn't enough for Julia to know *how* each dish was prepared—she wanted to understand the "why" behind each dish, too. Why were the ingredients coming together (or not) in certain ways? What were the factors that influenced the taste and texture of each dish? She appreciated the art of cooking, but she wanted to approach it logically and scientifically, too. In fact, she even referred to herself as a "mad scientist."

Take mayonnaise, for example. In theory, it was simple: beat olive oil into egg yolks, add a little salt and vinegar, and that's that. Julia had made it perfectly lots of times. But after a few months, the same techniques and ingredients started giving her trouble. The blend kept separating, making a thin and disgusting mess. Julia was determined to figure out what was going wrong. She went back to the beginning, testing each step, studying it all scientifically, writing everything down. "I made so much mayonnaise that Paul and I could hardly bear to eat it anymore," she wrote, "and I took to dumping my test batches down the toilet. What a shame." She finally figured out that the problem was the weather. It was winter, and her chilly kitchen had lowered the temperature of her bowl. For mayonnaise to come together properly, she discovered, everything needed to be room temperature—the ingredients *and* the equipment. With the thrill of victory, Julia typed up her perfect mayonnaise recipe and sent it to friends and family back home.

Nobody cared.

But the process of solving the mayonnaise problem appealed to Julia. It was the same methodical thinking and attention to detail that she had developed during the war. Only now, instead of organizing classified information for the OSS, she was using those skills for something she loved—writing foolproof recipes for delicious French meals.

CHAPTER EIGHT
"A Colossal Job"

As winter rolled into spring of 1950, Julia was losing patience with Le Cordon Bleu. Because of the school's financial problems, instructors and students didn't have key ingredients they needed. She was also frustrated with the other students in her class; after six months, they still couldn't properly clean a chicken. "They just weren't serious, and that irritated me," she wrote.

Julia decided to take a leave of absence from the school, working privately with Chef Bugnard at her home and continuing to practice, practice, practice what she'd been learning. She and Paul hosted countless dinner parties for friends, embassy staff, and visiting family members. All that entertaining allowed Julia to practice complicated dishes like stuffed veal with sauce, soufflés, and rich hearty stews made with all kinds of meat and game. Her expertise was growing every day. By late 1950, after a year of intensive cooking at school and at home, Julia earned her diploma. She was officially a graduate of Le Cordon Bleu.

While in school, Julia had joined an eating club called Le Cercle de Gourmettes, a group of women who met regularly to watch a professional cooking lesson and then, of course, to eat what was cooked. Julia loved this group, made up mainly of older women who had no patience for dainty nibbles and modest helpings—they had appetites as hearty as Julia's. It was social, it was French, and it centered around food. Julia was in heaven!

It was through this group that Julia got to know Simone Beck Fischbacher, a "tall, dashing, vigorous" French woman about Julia's age. They'd met once before at a party and quickly learned they shared a common obsession—food—so they'd agreed to get together more often. Simca, as Simone was known, introduced Julia to another French woman who loved to cook, Louisette Bertholle. Together, the three women tossed around the idea of starting a small cooking school—nothing fancy, just a few students at a time in one of their kitchens.

Julia floated the idea around the American Embassy, where there were plenty of women with both money and time to spare. Before Julia, Simca, and Louisette had even thought out their teaching strategies, students had signed up. Ah, well. Julia wasn't one to let that stop her. "[I]s anyone ever completely ready for a new undertaking, especially in a profession like cooking, where there are at least a hundred ways to cook a potato?" she wrote.

They called their school L'École de Trois Gourmandes— roughly translated as "the School of the Three Hearty Eaters." Their goal was to teach the techniques of French cuisine to American women who already enjoyed cooking and knew their way around a kitchen. Julia wanted to teach her students that the recipes weren't mysterious or impossible, not if you knew the basics. To do this, she needed to adapt the recipes into ones that Americans would be able to follow with the ingredients and methods available to them.

Julia loved teaching. Cooking in front of an audience brought out her inner performer. But she also enjoyed the attention to detail the classes demanded. She prided herself on making sure the recipes were exactly right, every time, and clearly communicated. It was complicated work—Europeans measured ingredients using the metric system, with grams and liters, and Julia had to convert all the recipes into the more familiar teaspoons and cups used by Americans. She also had to understand the differences between French and American ingredients. American flour, for example, had more gluten than French flour, which meant piecrusts needed more fat to bake properly. Julia, Simca, and Louisette experimented until they got the ratio of butter to flour just right. "Getting recipes into scientific workability is very interesting," Julia wrote to her sister-in-law.

Simca and Louisette were hoping their relationship with Julia would extend beyond teaching. A publisher in the United States had agreed to produce a French cookbook for Americans using Simca and Louisette's recipes, but it wasn't going well. Their editors thought the book was as dry as an overdone steak, and it didn't explain the reasons behind the French methods well enough. "Get an American who is crazy about French cooking to collaborate with you," they were told. "Somebody who both knows French food and can still . . . explain things with an American viewpoint in mind."

Somebody like Julia.

"I'd be delighted to!" she told them, when they finally worked up the nerve to ask her.

"It'll be a colossal job," Paul said as Julia poured over the manuscript during the summer of 1952. He was right. The more Julia looked at what Simca and Louisette had done, the less she liked it. It was a "big jumble of recipes" with complicated directions written in spotty English. "[I] knew from firsthand experience how frustrating it could be to try to learn from badly written recipes," she wrote. This book, as it was, wouldn't do at all.

They'd need to start over. From scratch.

Still, the project "fired [her] imagination." Simca and Louisette were talented cooks with a deep understanding of French cuisine. Many of the recipes they'd included came from their family collections. With a total rewrite, focused on clear explanations and well-tested directions, the book could be something really special.

Julia brought her incredible energy and work ethic to this project, much the way she had done as a student at Le Cordon Bleu. She tackled the soup chapter first, one soup every day. She'd start by testing Simca and Louisette's recipe, often several times. Then she'd prepare the same soup from recipes in other classic French cookbooks, working until she had the perfect dish. She took nothing for granted—no wives' tale, no bit of kitchen folk wisdom would go into her book unless it had been proven absolutely, factually true in her own experience. She would cook for eight, ten, fourteen hours a day and then type up the results on her trusty Underwood typewriter late into the night.

Julia happily kept up this routine all through the fall of 1952. "I had decided that cookbook writing was just the right job for me," she wrote later. "I found myself working for entire days on the manuscript with hardly a break. The house was becoming a wreck, but I hardly noticed." Simca and Julia worked together and separately on the recipes. Simca didn't understand Julia's need to test and retest everything, but she adapted to Julia's working style. For family reasons, Louisette didn't put in the number of hours that Julia and Simca did, but she provided input as well. They were, for the most part, a good team.

The publisher had not given them a contract—or any form of payment—and that bothered Julia. She was a savvy business-woman, and she worried that the publisher was taking advantage of all of their hard work and time, not to mention the small fortune they'd spent on ingredients. So Julia wrote her friend Avis DeVoto in Cambridge, Massachusetts, describing the situation they were in and sending her a draft of the sauce chapter.

Julia's friendship with Avis had started six months earlier. After reading a magazine article about crummy American knives that didn't cut anything, Julia sent the author, Bernard DeVoto, a letter and a French knife she was quite happy with. Avis, Bernard's wife, wrote a lovely letter back to to Julia, and so began a deep friendship between the two women. It was a lucky thing for Julia because Avis was a smart woman, was an accomplished cook, and had lots of friends in the publishing industry.

Avis read the sauce chapter and wrote Julia back on Christmas Day, 1952. "[Y]our manuscript came yesterday and I am wildly excited. . . . [I] am absolutely convinced that you have got something here that could be a classic and make your fortune and go on selling forever." She told Julia that she wanted to show the book to another publisher, Houghton Mifflin. Avis thought they would do a better job with it.

With Avis's help, Julia and her team had a contract the very next month. Houghton Mifflin would produce the book, pay Julia and her coauthors for their time working on it to this point, and assign an editor to the project—someone who would guide them through the writing and revising. Julia might not be a "lady novelist," but she was officially a writer—a cookbook writer. "Hooray!" she said.

The work was still difficult. And it was about to get even harder; in March 1953, Julia and Paul got word they'd have to pack up and move to Marseille, a town on the southern coast of France. Julia was devastated. She loved Paris so much that it broke her heart to leave. Packing and moving would force her out of the kitchen for a while, and the distance it would put between Julia and her coauthors would make it harder to collaborate. But moving was part of life in the Foreign Service. At least they'd still be in France, she told herself, as she packed up pages and pages of her cookbook manuscript and notes. Her papers and typewriter filled two huge steamer trunks, without an inch to spare!

CHAPTER NINE
Cook, Write, Move, Repeat

Julia had just started revising the chapter about fish before she and Paul left Paris. Lucky for her, their new apartment in Marseille was right next door to a fish market. She spent hours learning about the different kinds of fish and researching their American equivalents, even writing letters to the U.S. Department of Fisheries to get more information. If it was possible, Julia worked even harder on the book in Marseille. "She's determined to be author, foreign-service wife, cook, bottle washer, market buyer and sophisticated hostess," Paul wrote, amazed by her energy.

That energy would carry Julia through three moves in five years—to Germany, the United States, and Norway. After each move, she'd have to settle into her new kitchen, find the right ingredients, and continue the detailed process of testing and rewriting. She wrote page after typewritten page—drafts of the recipes themselves, letters to friends and family in the United States who were testing her recipes and providing feedback, and countless letters to Simca. (Louisette was not very involved in the book at this point.)

Julia's years with the OSS came in handy. She made sure to label her recipes "TOP SECRET" and insisted her testers not breathe a word about them to anyone. She didn't want them stolen and published by someone else!

Before their relocation to Germany, Paul and Julia took some vacation time back in the States. Julia finally met her pen pal, Avis, and their friendship grew even stronger. "I never had anybody in my house who was so completely effortless and easy, and whom I am so eager to see again," Avis wrote after Julia and Paul visited her in Cambridge. The feeling was mutual.

During Julia's two years in Pittlesdorf, Germany, she continued to cook and revise her recipes. Though she didn't like the military housing provided to Americans working there, the local grocery did carry American ingredients, which made it easier for Julia to test her recipes. The cookbook was growing every day, and Julia figured she and Simca had at least another year and a half, maybe two, before it would be finished. She used her time to focus on the meat and poultry chapters. She also practiced cooking on an electric stove—something she hated but needed to understand.

Paul was reassigned to a post in the States in 1956, and he and Julia moved back to their house in Washington, D.C. They gave it a total makeover, including their kitchen. The six-burner gas stove they bought was such a hit, Julia swore she'd take it with her to her grave. They entertained often, reconnecting with old friends.

But there was a trend Julia noticed back in her home country that troubled her. Many Americans weren't really cooking, she noticed, at least not in the way Julia would have them cook. Commercials and advertisements showed housewives who were so busy with their children that they had no time, or no desire, to make delicious meals from scratch. According to television and magazines, the "chauffeur-den-mother" woman wanted easy meals made with off-the-shelf ingredients—frozen vegetables, heat-and-eat dinners in metal tins, canned soups—nothing like the recipes Julia was writing.

If this was the way people were cooking, her book would be tough to sell. "I am deeply depressed, gnawed by doubts, and feel that all our work may just lay a big rotten egg," Julia wrote Avis. But she'd come too far to stop now. And anyway, when did Julia ever let other people keep her from doing something she enjoyed? If she loved French cooking this much, perhaps a few other people would, too. She continued working on the book during her time in Washington and during their final overseas post in Norway.

In the summer of 1959, seven years after starting the book, Julia sent a complete draft to her editor at Houghton Mifflin. It was a monster of a manuscript—750 pages long, now titled *French Recipes for American Cooks*. The book had occupied so much of her life for so long that the break from it felt strange. "[Y]ou'd think I'd be tripping about in ecstatic jubilation," she wrote. "But I felt rootless. Empty. Lost."

In November, Julia received a letter from Houghton Mifflin with devastating news: The book was too long and would be too expensive to produce. They weren't sure that American cooks would buy a hefty book filled with time-consuming recipes. It was too big a risk for the publisher to take—if the book didn't sell, they would lose a lot of money. "Believe me," the publisher's letter to Julia said, "I know how much work has gone into this manuscript. I send you my best wishes for its success elsewhere."

Julia's worst nightmare had come true. Her work *had* laid "a big, rotten egg," for exactly the reasons she feared it would. All that time, all that work—for nothing! Julia was crushed, not only for herself, but for Simca and Louisette, too. "You just picked the wrong American to collaborate with," she wrote them.

In her typical way, Julia tried to focus on the positives. She had completed this extremely challenging project to her own tough standards, for one thing. And she now had a fantastic collection of recipes to work from for the next phase in her career. What would that next phase be? She'd have to figure it out.

But Avis—good old Avis!—hadn't given up. She knew the book was too special to sit in a drawer. "We have only begun to fight," she wrote Julia. Then, without Julia or Simca knowing, Avis sent their manuscript to another publishing company, Knopf, where it landed on the desk of a young editor named Judith Jones.

There couldn't have been a more perfect editor for this project. Judith had lived in France, loved French cooking, and could see right away how different—how amazing—Julia's cookbook really was. She took pages home and started cooking from them. She had a dinner party where she made Julia's *boeuf bourguignon* (a complex, slow-cooked beef dish). The only problem with the meal was that the guests gobbled it up and wanted more!

This book was a treasure, and Judith knew a treasure when she saw one. She had experience rescuing great books from the trash bin. Years before, while living in France, Judith had worked as an assistant to a publisher, answering the mail and tending the office. One day, her boss asked her to throw away a pile of manuscripts that the company didn't want to publish. Judith picked one up and started reading, and she didn't stop until she'd finished the whole thing. "We have to get this to New York," Judith told her boss. "This has to be published." The book? Anne Frank's *The Diary of a Young Girl*, the haunting true story of a Jewish girl's experience hiding from the Nazis during World War II—now a classic.

Judith had the same feeling about Julia's manuscript when it crossed her desk in 1960. "There was nothing like it," Judith said in a later interview. "It was a unique book, and it changed the way that we think about cookbooks." Just as she had with *The Diary of a Young Girl*, Judith told her bosses, "We've got to publish this book!" They were skeptical, but they agreed.

In May 1960, Judith sent a letter to Julia in Norway. "Once again," Julia remembered, "I found myself holding a letter from a publisher that I hardly dared to open." But this letter held good news—Judith Jones wanted to publish the book!

It needed a better title, though. *French Recipes for American Cooks* wasn't snazzy enough, Judith thought, and Julia agreed. What would they call it? Julia and Simca had tried on lots of titles, but none of them fit. *The Noble Art of French Cooking?* No. *Cooking from the American Supermarket?* No. *French Magicians in the Kitchen?* No! *The Witchcraft of French Cooking?* Heavens, no!

Julia and Paul made lists of words at home. Judith did the same. It took months, but finally Judith found a title that said everything it needed to: *Mastering the Art of French Cooking*.

"You've got it," Julia told her.

Judith's boss had a different thought. "I'll eat my hat if anyone buys a book with that title," he grumped.

Julia didn't let his attitude get her down. Too many wonderful things were happening. Paul was retiring from the State Department, and he and Julia were moving back to the United States for good. They'd decided to settle in Cambridge and bought a lovely home on Irving Street, not far from Avis. Perhaps even more exciting was that, after years of hard work and the sting of rejection, Julia's book was almost a reality. She couldn't wait to see the finished product, to hold it in her hands and show it to the world. A new chapter of her life was beginning.

Cambridge, Massachusetts
1961

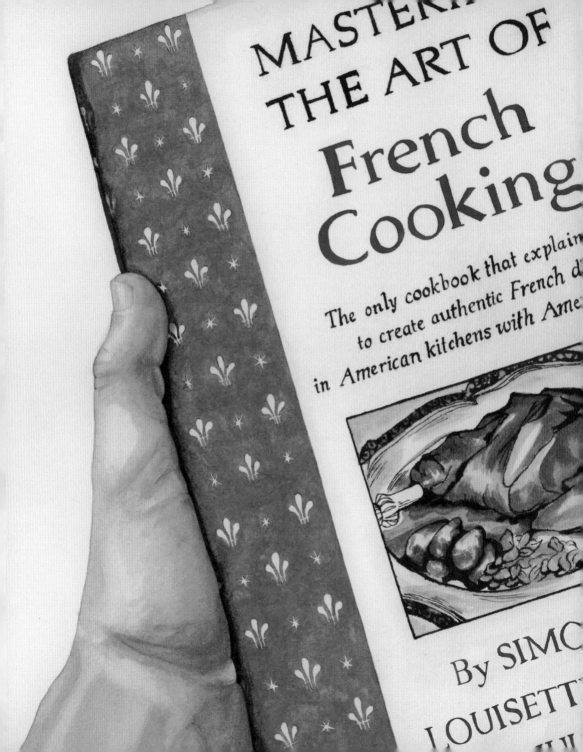

MASTERI
THE ART OF
French
Cooking

The only cookbook that explain
to create authentic French di
in American kitchens with Ame

By SIMO
LOUISETT

240

ROASTING TIMETABLE - OVEN TEMPERATURE: 350 DEGREES

READY-TO COOK WEIGHT	UNDRAWN WEIGHT (DRESSED WEIGHT)	NUMBER OF PEOPLE SERVED	APPROXIMATE TOTAL COOKING TIME
3/4 lb.	1 lb.	1 or 2	30 to 40 minutes
1 1/4 lbs.	2 lbs	2	40 to 50 minutes
2 lbs.	3 lbs	2 or 3	50 to 60 minutes
3 lbs.	4 lbs	4	1 hour and 10 to 20 minutes
4 lbs.	5 lbs.	4 or 5	1 hour and 15 to 30 minutes
4 1/2 lbs.	6 lbs.	5 or 6	1 hour and 25 to 40 minutes
5 1/4 lbs.	7 lbs	6 or 8	1 hour and 30 to 45 minutes

ROAST CHICKEN

✳ POULET RÔTI

[Roast Chicken]

You can always judge the quality of a cook or a restaurant by roast chicken. While it does not require years of training to produce a juicy, brown, buttery, crisp-skinned heavenly bird, it does entail such a greed for perfection that one is under compulsion to hover over the bird, listen to it above all see that it is continually basted, and that it is done just to the proper turn. Spit roasting, where the chicken is wrapped in fat and continually rotated, is fat less exacting than oven roasting where you must constantly turn and baste.

Small French chickens are frequently roasted without a stuffing. The cavity is seasoned with salt and butter, and the skin rubbed with butter. For oven roasting, it is browned lightly for 10 to 15 minutes at a temperature of 425 degrees, then the temperature is reduced to 350, and the chicken is turned and basted until it is done. A simple, short deglazing sauce is made with stock — about a tablespoonful for each serving.

241

ROAST CHICKEN

One of the potato casseroles on page 523, and green peas or beans
Stuffed mushrooms, glazed carrots, and glazed onions
Ratatouille (eggplant casserole), page 503, and sautéed potatoes

WINE SUGGESTIONS

A light red wine, such as a Bordeaux-Médoc, or a rosé

For 4 people

Estimated roasting time for a 3 pound chicken: 1 hour and 10 to 20 minutes

Preheat oven to 425 degrees

A 3-lb., ready-to-cook roasting or frying chicken
1/4 tsp salt
2 Tb softened butter

Sprinkle the inside of the chicken with the salt, and smear in half the butter. Truss the chicken, page 237. Dry it thoroughly, and rub the skin with the rest of the butter.

A shallow roasting pan just large enough to hold the chicken easily
To flavor the sauce: a small sliced carrot and onion
For basting a small sauce pan containing 2 Tb melted butter, 1 Tb good cooking oil; a basting brush

Place the chicken breast up in the roasting pan. Strew the vegetables around it, and set it on a rack in the middle of the preheated oven. Allow the chicken to brown lightly for 15 minutes, turning it on the left side after 5 minutes, on the right side for the last 5 minutes, and basting it with the butter and oil after each turn. Baste rapidly, so oven does not cool off. Reduce oven to 350 degrees. Leave the chicken on its side, and baste every 8 to 10 minutes, using the fat in the roasting pan when the butter and oil are exhausted. Regulate oven heat so chicken is making cooking noises, but fat is not burning.

1/4 tsp salt

Halfway through estimated roasting time, salt the chicken and turn it on its other side. Continue basting

1/4 tsp salt

Fifteen minutes before end of estimated roasting time, salt again and turn the chicken breast up. Continue basting.

Indications that the chicken is almost done are: a sudden ... splutters in the oven, a swelling of the ... drumstick is

CHAPTER TEN
Flying Off the Shelves

Julia could hardly believe it. After years of testing and retesting, writing and rewriting, she had wondered if this moment would ever come. But here it was, all 732 pages of it. Julia admired the black and red title, the cover decorated with a picture of a roast with vegetables and sprinkled with little French fleurs-de-lis along the side. Julia loved the fact that, no matter what page you opened to, the book would rest flat on a kitchen counter. Cooks wouldn't have to worry about holding down the pages while they worked. The book was "perfectly beautiful in every respect," she said.

Boxes needed unpacking, and their Irving Street kitchen needed a remodel, but all of that would have to wait. Suddenly life got very busy—it was time to make sure the world knew about *Mastering the Art of French Cooking*.

To do that, Julia and Simca planned a publicity tour. They contacted everyone they knew in several major cities, offering to give interviews and demonstrations, meet booksellers and book reviewers, chat with restaurant people and food writers. They'd spend time with anyone and everyone who might help them encourage people to buy their book.

They started in New York. Simca flew in from France, where she met Julia and Paul for ten days of book-related events in

New York City. Julia didn't know what to expect. "I had no idea how to arrange for publicity," she remembered later. "Besides, I hated the whole idea of selling ourselves."

The job of "selling themselves" was easier than they thought it would be. Two days after the book was released, they received a review in the *New York Times*. A good review in a well-known newspaper helps books sell lots of copies. And the review of Julia's book wasn't just good—it was fantastic! "The recipes are glorious. . . ." the reviewer wrote. "All [the recipes] are . . . written as if each were a masterpiece, and most of them are." The only criticisms of the book were that some recipes required a garlic press (the reviewer thought that the tool cheapened the taste of garlic) and that the authors hadn't included a recipe for puff pastry. Still, "[w]e couldn't have written a better review ourselves," Julia said later.

The book launch was off to a good start, and it got even better a few days later when Julia and Simca appeared on NBC's *Today* show. Television at this time was still pretty new (Julia and Paul didn't even own one), and it was an exciting opportunity. Four million people watched the *Today* show every morning. Imagine introducing the book to that many people at once!

Julia and Simca were given a five-minute time slot and decided to do a cooking demonstration. The most exciting dish they could pull off in that short time was an omelette. They showed up at the station at five o'clock in the morning, lugging three dozen eggs, knives, bowls, and pans. There was only one problem, and it was a big one.

The "stove" the station promised them turned out to be just a weak hot plate. "The [darned] thing just wouldn't heat up properly for an omelette," Julia moaned. During the hour they had to wait, they made omelette after runny omelette, trying to find a solution. What could they do? If the pan wasn't hot enough during their demonstration, they'd have to fake it somehow.

Five minutes before the interview began, Julia and Simca put their omelette pan on the hot plate and left it there to get as hot as it could. While they filmed, the host of the show made them feel relaxed and comfortable, and Julia enjoyed the conversation. And luckily enough, when the time came for the demonstration, the pan was hot. "By heaven, if that one last omelette didn't work out perfectly!" Julia remembered.

Maybe it was her experience performing in plays in her youth, or maybe it was the fact that Julia felt relaxed and at ease anywhere, but while Simca faded into the background, Julia glowed on television. "Almost immediately, she was so comfortable on TV," said her niece Rachel, who watched the interview from the studio.

The next day, Julia and Simca were scheduled to do a cooking demonstration at a department store. This kind of event usually attracted a few shoppers passing by, but hundreds of people came to watch Julia and Simca, almost surely a result of their *Today* show appearance. By the end of that first week, Julia wrote a letter to her sister. "The old book seems, for some happy reason, to have caught on here in New York, and our publishers are beginning to think they have a modest best seller on their hands."

Earlier, Judith's boss had said he'd "eat his hat" if anyone bought a book called *Mastering the Art of French Cooking*. Was there a recipe for cooking a hat in that massive cookbook of Julia's?

Julia, Paul, and Simca traveled to Detroit, San Francisco, Los Angeles, Washington, and back to New York to promote the book. Julia and Simca did radio interviews, went to parties and teas in their honor, gave talks at bookstores, did cooking demonstrations at department stores, and met with anyone who might influence newspapers and magazines to write about their book. It was an exhausting six weeks.

Paul worked as hard as Julia and Simca did, just behind the scenes. His years spent designing and planning exhibits and events was a huge help. Paul was the one who could focus on the tables and the equipment, the microphones and stage lights, all the little details that go into a successful presentation. Once, after a cooking demonstration at a department store in New York, Judith Jones went to the ladies' room. There was Paul, washing pots and pans in the tiny bathroom sink, "happy as a clam!"

The events were wildly successful. People lined up to see Julia and Simca's cooking demonstrations, and their book often sold out of the bookstores where they presented. Judith Jones was amazed. She said that "authors in those days didn't draw that kind of audience." What was it about *Mastering the Art of French Cooking* that people were connecting with? What happened to those "chauffeur-den-mothers" who only wanted quick and easy recipes?

Luckily for Julia, the same year her book came out, the newly elected president, John F. Kennedy Jr., and his wife, Jacquelyn Bouvier Kennedy, moved into the White House. The Kennedys were a young, glamorous couple known for their fine taste in food and clothes, and many people wanted to be as sophisticated as they were. The Kennedys hired the White House's first French chef, a man named René Verdun. This put French cooking in the news, something that certainly helped bring attention to Julia's book.

But a French chef in the White House couldn't explain everything. Something else brought people to those recipes. Perhaps some American cooks were tired of boring, prepackaged meals. Maybe they were ready to spend a little more time on food that was delicious. Maybe they wanted to make dinners they could be proud to serve their families and friends.

Given the way her book was flying off the shelves, Julia's approach to cooking was clearly something Americans were hungry for.

CHAPTER ELEVEN
The Madwoman Cooks an Omelette

With the book tour successfully completed, things settled down a little. Julia and Paul headed home to Cambridge. They took on that kitchen remodel, making the counters taller so Julia could cook more comfortably and adding storage for her pots and pans. Just like he'd done in France, Paul drew an outline of every hanging utensil on a pegboard so Julia would know exactly where everything went. She called this kitchen a "real *wowzer*."

Julia's cookbook had sold enough copies to start earning her some money, and she and Paul used her first check to buy (among other things) their first television set. Julia thought the television was so ugly that she hid it in an unused fireplace. She had no idea then how much television would impact her life, or how much she would impact television.

Today, anyone with a cable subscription can flip through hundreds of channels airing shows twenty-four hours a day. But when Julia bought her first television set, only three channels—CBS, NBC, and ABC—were broadcast across the country. Those stations didn't have enough programs to be on the air all day long. Television producers were still figuring out what kinds of shows worked in this new medium.

In February of 1962, Julia received an invitation to appear on a show called *I've Been Reading* on the Boston public television station, WGBH. WGBH was different from the three more popular national stations. It was a local educational channel that aired shows featuring Boston-based authors and university professors. One of the crew members of *I've Been Reading* called the show "dry as toast," and not many people watched it.

When Julia called the station and said, "Now, dearie, I will require a hot plate for my appearance on [the] program," the producer, Russ Morash, didn't know what to think. "You've got a hot one here this week," Russ told his assistant.

But Julia couldn't imagine doing the interview any other way. "Educational television was just talking heads," she said later, "and I did not know what we would talk about for that long, so I brought the eggs." Just like she had for the *Today* show (but with a working hot plate!) Julia whipped eggs and sliced mushrooms, showing viewers proper omelette techniques while she chatted comfortably with the host. Behind her was a blown-up copy of her book's cover. Russ couldn't believe what he was seeing. "I thought to myself: Who is this madwoman cooking an omelette on a book-review program?"

No one at WGBH could have imagined the response to Julia's demonstration. Her appearance on *I've Been Reading* was such a success that twenty-seven people wrote letters to the station. Twenty-seven letters may not sound like a lot, but it certainly made the staff at WGBH sit up and take notice. "I don't think one of [the letters] mentioned our book," Julia wrote later, "but they *did* say things like 'Get that woman back on television. We want to see some more cooking!'"

Russ and the other producers started to wonder if Julia could pull off an entire show. This was a pretty radical idea for the time. There had been only two national cooking shows before, and neither of them did very well. But there was something about Julia, something about the way she had so much fun cooking on camera. They invited her to shoot three pilot episodes, a trial run to see how viewers responded. Depending on how those went, they offered her the possibility of a full year's worth of shows. Her own cooking show!

Julia wasn't sure at first. "I knew nothing at all about television," she wrote later. But she liked the fact that the station was an educational channel. She saw television as a way to teach. Who knew, maybe it would build excitement for a cooking school she might open one day. "We knew this was a great opportunity for . . . *something*, none of us was exactly sure what," she wrote.

Sitting around the kitchen table in the Irving Street house, Julia, Paul, and the WGBH television producers—Russ Morash and his assistant, Ruth Lockwood—mapped out the first three shows. Each episode would focus on one dish, something interesting but not too complicated. The three dishes they'd film would be the omelette, a chicken stew called *coq au vin*, and a dessert called a soufflé.

They decided that each show should have the same structure. First, Julia would introduce the dish and the ingredients. Then she'd prepare the dish, explaining all the steps. For the finale, Julia would take the finished dish into a dining room, where she would sit at a table with candles and wine and taste what she'd made.

Julia and Paul began rehearsing at home. She broke down the recipes into logical steps, taking detailed notes about what she should be saying and doing at each point in the program, along with a running list of the ingredients and equipment she'd need for each step. Paul took notes, too. He made drawings showing where everything—even the dishtowels—would be located on the set. He wrote instructions to himself. "At the finish of the omelettete series, remove French pan...bowl, whip, cup and green plate." Just like on the book tour, Paul would be a key behind-the-scenes ingredient to the success of Julia's show.

While Julia and Paul rehearsed, Russ and Ruth also got to work. There was no time (and no money) to build a new set for Julia's show. Luckily, Russ found out that the local gas company had a model kitchen set up to demonstrate how to use gas-powered stoves. With a few homey touches, like curtains over the fake windows, Russ and Ruth made it look like a real kitchen (minus the running water).

The next challenge was a familiar one: What would they name the show? That pesky title was as tricky for the television show as it had been for Julia's cookbook! The perfect title had to be catchy enough to remember, short enough to fit in the printed TV guides, and informative enough to tell viewers what to expect. Dozens of ideas flew back and forth before Ruth finally came up with the one that stuck: *The French Chef.*

They had a title and a set. But the question still remained: Would they have any viewers?

CHAPTER TWELVE
"Bon Appétit!"

On the morning of June 18, 1962, after weeks of rehearsing, Julia and Paul loaded up their car with everything they'd need for the first show—the omelette episode—and headed to the Boston Gas Company. Imagine how confused the executives and their secretaries must have been to see Julia and Paul whisking through their lobby, weighed down by bowls, bags of ingredients, and cartons of eggs!

In the basement demonstration kitchen, Julia, Paul, Russ, and Ruth made their final preparations—setting up the cameras and lights and checking the sound. Some of the television equipment had to operate from an enormous bus that was parked outside, with cords running into the building from the parking lot. The cameramen had never worked on a cooking show, and they barely knew their way around a kitchen. When Russ, from his command station in the bus, told one of them to get a close-up of the garlic press, the cameraman shot back with, "What the [heck] is a garlic press?"

The shows weren't live, but they were filmed as if they were. Editing video in those days was a complicated and expensive job. Unless something went horribly wrong, the cameras would keep rolling. "This was a bit of a high-wire act, but it suited me," Julia said later. Some mistakes could be good for the show. If the dish didn't turn out correctly, Julia could teach her viewers how to correct it.

They'd prepared everything they could. Now it was time to shoot! Julia spread her notes around the kitchen, got her ingredients into place, and took a deep breath.

"And, action!"

"Hello, I'm Julia Child," she began. And off she went, talking her viewers through each step of a perfect omelette. Her warm and warbly voice sounded like she was talking to a friend instead of a huge camera. When the filming ended, her skin was flushed from the hot stage lights and she felt a little breathless, but the show came off without a hitch, garlic press and all.

The *coq au vin* and souflée shows were filmed a week later, both on the same day. Julia thought those went much better because she and Paul put in even more time rehearsing at home and she knew a little more what to expect. She worked on her breathing so that she wouldn't sound so winded during the show. At the end of the souflée episode, Julia sat at the table and poured herself a glass of wine. She showed the audience the dish she'd just made. She reminded the viewers who she was, thanked them, and then said warmly, "*Bon appétit!*"

It became Julia's signature phrase, two French words that would forever make people think of this famous American cook. *Bon appétit* literally means "good appetite," and it's said in French restaurants and homes as a dish is presented at the table. Roughly translated into English, it means "Enjoy your meal," but that sounds stuffy. When Julia said it at the end of every episode, it was an affectionate good-bye and a wish for her viewers to truly enjoy the pleasures of cooking and eating.

Her producers were thrilled with the first three episodes. "Julia sailed through the pilots," Russ said in a later interview. He called Julia a "joy to work with," partly because her performances were so organized, but mostly because she had a wonderful way about her on camera.

Would viewers at home feel the same way? "[W]ould there be an audience out there in TV Land for a cooking show hosted by one Julia McWilliams Child?" Julia wondered. She'd find out soon enough when the first show aired, about two weeks later.

On the big day, Julia cooked a steak dinner. It was so hot that she and Paul ate outside, electric fans rigged up to create some kind of a breeze. Then, at 8:30 p.m., they went inside, pulled the ugly television from its spot in the fireplace, and turned on channel 2.

"There I was in black and white, a large woman sloshing eggs too quickly here, too slowly there, gasping, looking at the wrong camera while talking too loudly, and so on," Julia said. She saw lots of room for improvement. She even wrote to a friend of hers that it would take twenty shows or more before she felt she knew what she was doing. But "Paul said I looked and sounded just like myself."

Viewers loved the pilot episodes. "We have been fascinated with the new program, '*The French Chef*,'" one person wrote just days after the episodes aired, "and very much hope that there will be more than three of these." Another fan wrote, "[T]his series deserves to get national distribution on the network." Several viewers included donations to the station with their letters. (Unlike the major networks that got money from advertising, educational channels like WGBH relied on money given by the viewers to stay on the air.) "[T]he excellence of Julia Child's *The French Chef* program has prompted me to send an additional small contribution," wrote one person. Letters were nice, but letters with donations? That definitely got the station's attention. WGBH quickly offered Julia the chance to film a full season, twenty-six episodes that would air in the winter of 1963.

Her first full season of *The French Chef* was loads of work. Julia would spend all weekend at home writing the script, buying the ingredients, and rehearsing with Paul. Then she'd tape two shows a day at the studio—twelve-hour days!

But all that hard work paid off. By July of 1964, WGBH was receiving between 300 and 400 fan letters a week for Julia, not to mention the letters pouring into the other stations in other cities airing her show—New York, Philadelphia, and Pittsburgh, to name a few. Thirty-three educational stations carried *The French Chef* that fall, and a few months later it would air on all of the eighty-five educational stations across the country.

The Set of *The French Chef*
1970

WG

THE FR

206

TAKE:

ONE

SERIES:

TWO

To

4

EPISO

BH-TV

NCH CHEF

RoastAChicken

6-70 | T.B.A.

WO

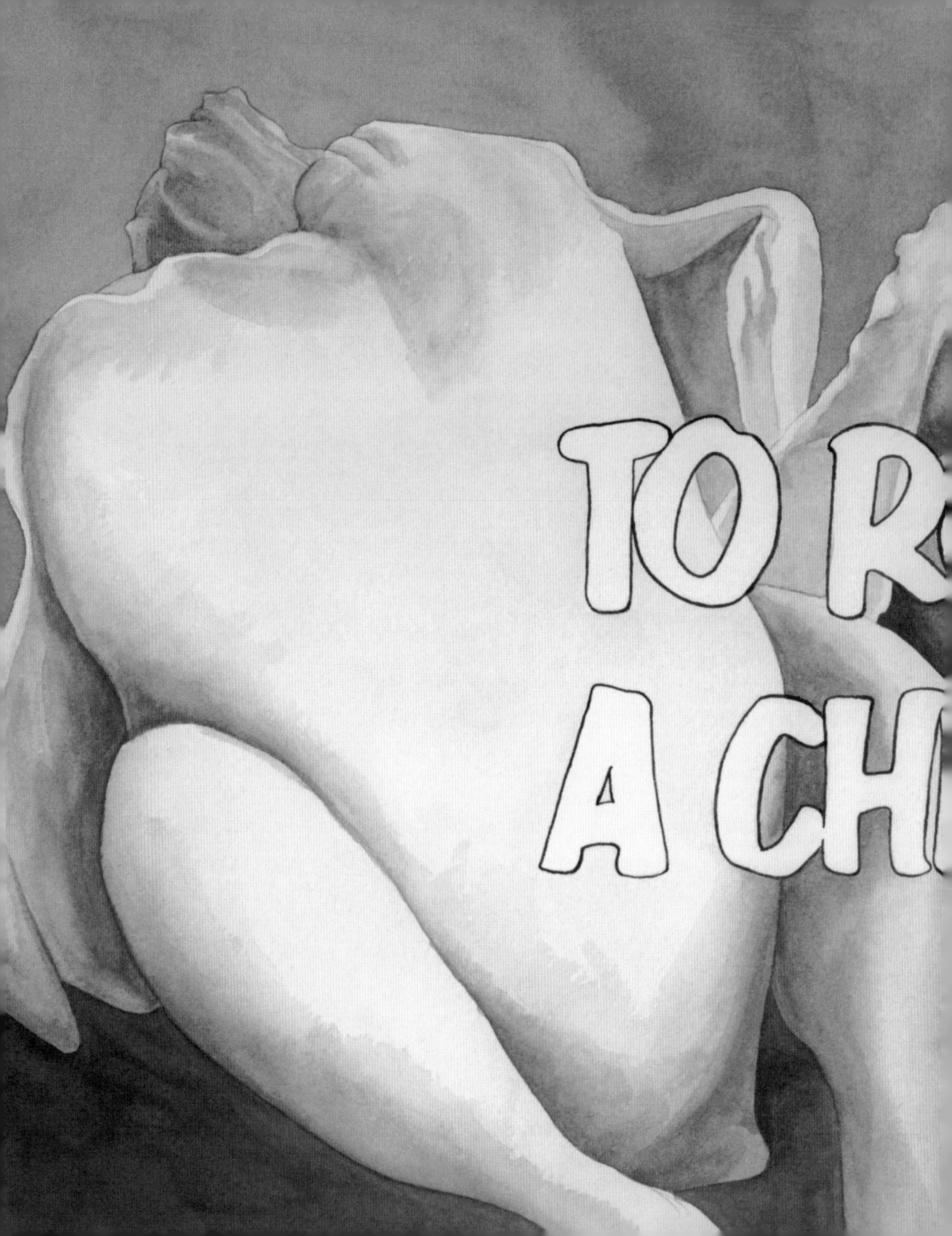
TO R
A CH

OAST
CKEN

CHAPTER THIRTEEN
A Legend in the Making

Why did viewers respond so well to Julia? Her personality was certainly one reason. People didn't feel like they were watching a television star or a finicky chef doing things in the kitchen that they could never hope to do. Julia felt familiar, like a favorite aunt who had come for a visit to show you how to cook something delicious. There was nothing stuffy or uptight about watching her. She played with her ingredients, made jokes, and closed her eyes and cooed when she tasted something delicious.

Time and time again, Julia showed her viewers that she wasn't a magician. She was just a regular person who'd learned to cook this way, and they could, too. In one episode, she demonstrated how to tie up a chicken before roasting it, a process that looked like sewing the raw bird closed. She described how she'd "looked all over town" for a special needle. She couldn't find it, so she had Paul drill a hole in a knitting needle. "If you don't have a handyman at home, ask your dentist," she suggested. "They like drilling things." She put on her glasses to thread the needle, the way many fifty-year-old people need to do. As she wove the string in and out of the chicken, her hands were strong and steady, not beautiful or manicured. Throughout the entire lesson, viewers saw the same Julia she'd been all her life—warm, comfortable, and confident.

Julia clearly knew what she was doing in the kitchen, but viewers loved the way little things went wrong on the show. It looked just the way things went wrong in their own kitchens! Julia turned many of these moments into learning opportunities. If her dishes didn't come out the way she wanted, she'd fix them, right there on camera. A sauce too thick? Add a little cream! Potato pancake falls onto the stove while you're trying to flip it? Pick it up, flatten it out, and bake it in the oven! "If you're alone in the kitchen, whoooo is going to see?" Julia asked. Then she instructed her viewers, "The only way you can learn to flip something is just to flip it."

In her show on French onion soup, her elbow knocked over a bottle of cooking wine. "Oh, there goes the brandy!" she said in that unique voice. "That's too bad." Even now, years later, people laugh when they see that. It's so human, so unrehearsed, so honest. Just like Julia herself.

All kinds of people wrote to tell Julia how her approach to cooking had impacted their lives. Men even wrote Julia fan letters, which was surprising since women were the primary cooks and homemakers during this time. Peter from Chicago wrote, "I never learned so much in a half-hour or had a subject presented so concisely and with so much information packed into so short a time. Miss Child, let me tell you, you're marvelous, the show is marvelous, and your knowledge and presentation of your subject astounds me. . . ."

Kids wrote Julia letters, too! A ten-year-old boy named Chris told her all about his interest in attending Le Cordon Bleu. A Girl Scout named Pam wrote to say that she watched *The French Chef* every week with her grandmother and thought it would surely help her earn her cooking badge. A seventh-grader from Delaware named Betsy told Julia that, because of the episode about lobsters the week before, Betsy had been the only student in her biology class who'd successfully dissected a crayfish.

Perhaps the most rewarding letters came from women like Mrs. Graham Geise in Kingston, Rhode Island, who described the way her young children crowded around her feet while she cooked. "This doesn't prevent me from trying out flaming soufflés, even though serving them to a tableful of preschoolers does seem ludicrous at times." This letter was from a real-life "chauffeur-den-mother." She was exactly the kind of woman Julia's original publisher thought would have no use for these recipes, and she was writing to say that Julia's book and television show had "added a new dimension to our life." She went on to say, "[Y]ou find in me one of your most devoted disciples."

The show became so popular that it caught the eye of the national commercial TV stations. Julia would have been paid a lot more money if she had brought her show over to these networks, but she turned them all down, choosing to remain on educational television. "I am a teacher and I'll stay with the educators," she said.

Julia could have also made a lot of money by using her show or her image to promote brands of food or cooking products, but she refused to do that, too. "I just don't want to be in any way associated with commercialism," she once said. She felt that her viewers wouldn't trust her if she acted like a salesperson for a particular blender or brand of spices.

But there was no denying that, because of her show, things sold. Grocery stores ran out of ingredients—even broccoli and artichokes—the day after she used them on her show. Department stores and hardware stores sold out of wire whisks after people watched Julia use them to beat egg whites.

One day, Paul went to the butcher to pick up some meat. He watched, amazed, as a woman walked in, pulled a well-worn copy of *Mastering the Art of French Cooking* from a shelf and flipped through it. Right there in the butcher shop, the woman made her shopping list from Julia's book, then waited in line for her turn to order. The butcher told Paul, "They *all* use it."

Paul wrote his brother, describing their "monstrously busy" lives and sharing news of Julia's many successes. Charlie wrote back, "Julie could get to be a legend."

How right he was.

CHAPTER FOURTEEN
"Keep Right On"

"I was 32 when I started cooking; up until then I just ate," Julia Child is often quoted as saying. It took years for Julia to find her passion. But once she did, she grabbed hold and gave it every ounce of her incredible energy. Learning the techniques of French cooking, writing and rewriting the recipes for her book, planning and producing her television show—it was exhausting work, but it was work that brought Julia much joy.

In 1966, *Time* magazine put a painting of Julia on its cover, calling her the "Lady of the Ladle." That same year, *The French Chef* won an Emmy Award for its achievement in educational television. The success of the show boosted the sales of Julia's book, too. By the time she'd won the Emmy, the book had sold well over 100,000 copies and was still going strong. At fifty-four years old, with this kind of success, Julia could have filmed another season or two of her show and settled down into a quiet routine of teaching cooking classes and making an occasional speech. She and Paul had already built a second home in France, after all. It was the perfect place to retire.

But does that sound like Julia?

"Retired people are boring," she said. "In this line of work, you never have to retire. You keep right on until you are through." And that's just what Julia did.

She went on to publish *seventeen* cookbooks. Some critics thought that *Mastering the Art of French Cooking II*, which was written with Simca, was an even greater accomplishment than the first book. It included a twenty-one-page recipe for French bread that took Julia, with Paul's help, more than a year to research and write.

After that book, Julia decided that she preferred to write by herself rather than collaborate with Simca. The women were still good friends, but Simca drove Julia crazy by changing her mind about recipes or ingredients after she and Julia had already approved them.

Julia's last cookbook, *Julia's Kitchen Wisdom*, was published in 1999 when she was eighty-seven years old. Just as she had with *Mastering the Art of French Cooking*, Julia traveled the country to promote her book, sitting for hours while long lines of fans waited for the chance to have her sign their books. She made time to have a private moment with each fan, often asking, "Dearie, what is *your* favorite dish?" She loved signing worn-out, food-splattered copies of *Mastering* the best because she knew those books had done just what she'd intended: brought delicious meals into someone's home.

Julia was instrumental in pushing WGBH into the modern realm of color television. She thought her show would look too old-fashioned if it stayed in black and white, and the food would be much more appetizing in color. The color cameras were too expensive, the station argued, but Julia wouldn't budge. She was so important to the station that they finally agreed. Viewers who tuned into *The French Chef*'s 1970 season saw Julia's dishes in all their glorious colors. "Real strawberries look so much better than gray lumps," Julia said.

The French Chef aired until 1973. But that wasn't the end of Julia's TV career. She starred in seven more series, all on educational television. In many, she shared the spotlight with other chefs, and viewers loved watching Julia exchange ideas (and get in friendly disagreements) with them. Throughout all of these shows, viewers saw the same easygoing Julia they'd loved for years.

As he had been all along, Paul continued to be Julia's rock. He traveled with her, helped her on the sets of her television shows, and managed all the invitations she received until they got to be too much and she hired a secretary. Her dedication to him in her second cookbook said it all: "Paul Child, the man who is always there: porter, dishwasher, official photographer, mushroom dicer and onion chopper, editor, fish illustrator, manager, taster, idea man, resident poet, and husband." Paul died in May of 1994 after many years in a nursing home.

In 1992, when Julia turned eighty, there were thirty parties to celebrate. The biggest, fanciest one was held at the Ritz-Carlton Hotel in Los Angeles. Five hundred guests enjoyed a six-course French dinner prepared by sixty of the nation's best chefs. It took months to prepare, but what a perfect way to celebrate the queen of French cuisine!

Julia was still the most recognizable face of fine food, but even at this age she wasn't snobby about it. When she had friends for dinner, she always served one of her favorite snacks: Pepperidge Farm Goldfish crackers. She enjoyed hot dogs with sauerkraut as much as she enjoyed asparagus with hollandaise sauce. Just like always, she liked food that tasted good. Simple as that.

When Julia was eighty-nine, she announced her plan to move from Boston back to California. She still had family and friends out there, and she wanted to spend her final years in the beautiful place where she grew up. She gave her Irving Street house to Smith College, with one exception—the kitchen would be preserved at the Smithsonian Institute's Museum of American History in Washington, where it would be a permanent exhibit.

She enjoyed a simpler life in California, renting a small apartment in a retirement community. She got together with friends for breakfasts (where she often stole a few slices of bacon to make sandwiches later) and went out for dinners in Santa Barbara.

Julia's doctors told her she'd have to monitor her intake of butter and wine, but Julia just laughed and called them "silly boys!" She gave her caretaker fits, too. Stephanie Hersh had been Julia's personal assistant in Cambridge. Now, with Julia's health in decline, she drove Julia to appointments and tried to get her to follow the doctors' orders. But like a sneaky teenager, Julia would make plans for dinners with friends behind Stephanie's back, scooting past her on her way out the door with a cheery, "Don't wait up, dearie!"

In 2002, when she was ninety, Julia decided to work with her nephew, Alex Prud'homme, on a memoir about her years in France with Paul. *My Life in France* would be Julia's last book. That same year, President George W. Bush awarded her the Presidential Medal of Freedom, an award given to those individuals who have greatly impacted the nation's cultural interest. She wasn't well enough to travel, but she accepted his congratulations and the award over the phone.

Two nights before her ninety-second birthday, Julia made herself a pot of her favorite comfort food—one she'd introduced to Americans years before—French onion soup. She enjoyed two bowls and went to bed. When she woke up, she didn't feel right. She had an infection, her doctor said, and without treatment she'd die in days. Would her energy return to normal after treatment, she asked. The doctor said no.

So Julia refused the treatment. She'd lived her entire life on her own terms; why should the end be any different? "If I can't live the way I want to live," she told Stephanie, "I'd rather not live at all." Then she went upstairs to take a nap and died peacefully in her sleep.

Julia once said that "People who love to eat are always the best people." Clearly, anyone who has been touched by her throughout the years—family and friends, chefs and home cooks, food critics and butchers, almost anyone who's ever taken the time to enjoy a lovingly prepared dish—would agree that Julia Child was one of the best people. "To me," she said, "the kitchen has never stopped being a place just full of possibilities and pleasures." And thanks to Julia, many home cooks young and old feel exactly the same way.

Bon appétit, Julia!

Julia Child's Kitchen
National Museum of American History
Washington, D.C.
Present Day

NATIONAL MUSEUM OF AMERICAN HISTORY

Bon Appétit!
Julia Child's Kitchen
at the Smithsonian

Harbor Hotel
nue,
al district
0 or 439-3995

Julia Child's
handwritten Recipe

BIBLIOGRAPHY

BOOKS

Child, Julia, and Alex Prud'homme. *My Life in France*. New York: Anchor Books, 2007.

Fitch, Noel Riley. *Appetite for Life: The Biography of Julia Child*. New York: Anchor Books, 2012.

Karbo, Karen. *Julia Child Rules: Lessons on Savoring Life*. Guilford, CT: Skirt/Globe Pequot, 2013.

Reardon, Joan, ed. *As Always, Julia: The Letters of Julia Child and Avis DeVoto*. New York: Mariner Books, 2012.

Spitz, Bob. *Dearie: The Remarkable Life of Julia Child*. New York: Vintage Books, 2012.

OTHER SOURCES

Cheaklos, Christina. "Julia Child: 1912-2004." *People*, Vol. 62, No. 9, August 30, 2004.

Child, Julia. "Dedication" from *The French Chef Cookbook*. New York: Knopf, 1968.

Claiborne, Craig. "Cookbook Review: Glorious Recipes." *New York Times*, October 18, 1961. Web.

The French Chef, season 1, episode 2, "French Onion Soup"; season 1, episode 22, "The Potato Show"; season 1, episode 3, "Casserole Roast Chicken."

Hampson, Sarah. "Julia & Judith." *Globe and Mail*, July 26, 2009. Web.

Julia Child Papers, 1925-1993; MC 644. Schlesinger Library, Radcliffe Institute, Harvard University, Cambridge, Mass.

Julier, Alice. "Julia at Smith." *Gastronomica: The Journal of Food and Culture*, Vol. 5, No. 3, Summer 2005. Pp. 44–53.

Time, March 18, 2002, as told to Francine Russo.

GLOSSARY

academic Relating to school or college.

adolescent A person in the period of life from puberty to maturity.

allies Countries that join forces to fight together in a war.

anthropologist A person that studies human beings, their physical characteristics, their origin, their social relations, and their culture.

auxiliary A group that provides extra help to another group or organization.

braise To cook something slowly in fat and little moisture in a pot.

Buddhist Pertaining or relating to a religion of eastern and central Asia based on the teachings of Gautama Buddha.

eggs Florentine A dish of poached eggs over bread and spinach covered with a white sauce.

fleur-de-lis A French symbol that represents a lily.

hollandaise sauce A creamy sauce of melted butter, egg yolks, and lemon juice or vinegar.

intellectuals People interested in learning and thinking.

ladle A spoon with a long handle and a deep bowl used for serving soups.

lard A soft white fat that comes from pigs.

manuscript The written or typewritten composition for a book or document.

mortar A strong bowl in which food is crushed with a heavy tool called a pestle.

GLOSSARY

novelist — A writer who creates a work of literature with imaginary characters and events.

poultry — Birds, like chicken or turkey, raised for food.

quenelles de brochet — Soft, small cakes, usually made with fish and eggs.

rice paddies — Fields where rice is grown.

sauce Mornay — (*See* hollandaise sauce above) A hollandaise sauce that also has cheese.

shallot — A small vegetable with bulbs that resemble garlic; green onion.

sole muniere — A dish prepared by coating a type of fish called sole in milk and flour and frying it in butter.

soufflé — A lighty baked cake made with egg yolks and beaten egg whites.

succulent — Delicious, tasty.

veal — A young calf that is used for food.

TIMELINE

1912	Julia Carolyn McWilliams is born in Pasadena, California, on August 15
1935	Moves to New York City wanting to be a writer and finds a job at W. & J. Sloane
1937	Returns to California
1942	Starts working at the Office of Strategic Services in Washington, D.C.
1944	Transfers to Kandy, Ceylon, and meets Paul Child
1945	Transfers again to Kunming, China, where Paul also ends up; Julia and Paul return to the U. S. at the end of World War II
1946	Julia and Paul are married in Lumberville, Pennsylvania, in September
1948	Julia and Paul move to Paris for Paul's job with the U. S. Foreign Service
1949	Julia enrolls in Le Cordon Bleu cooking school
1952	Julia, Simca, and Louisette start their cooking school and begin collaborating on what will become *Mastering the Art of French Cooking*
1959	Julia, Simca, and Louisette finish the manuscript for their book; the project is rejected by Houghton Mifflin
1960	The manuscript is accepted for publication by Judith Jones at Alfred A. Knopf
1961	Paul retires from the Foreign Service and the Childs move to Cambridge, Massachusetts; *Mastering the Art of French Cooking* is published in October
1962	Julia appears on WGBH's *I've Been Reading*; *The French Chef* premieres, launching her television career and making her a household name
1994	Paul Child dies
2004	Julia Child dies on August 13

INDEX

ACKNOWLEDGMENTS

I am very grateful to the research librarians at the Arthur and Elizabeth Schlesinger Library on the History of Women in America for their assistance and their meticulous care of Julia Child's papers. Bob Spitz was kind enough to clarify some research questions early in the project, and his time is much appreciated. Like my own personal Avis DeVoto, Robin Pinto championed this book from afar and, with her thoughtful and encouraging correspondence, helped make it something I am very proud to have written. And none of this could have ever happened without my Paul, Paul Smith, every bit as helpful and supportive as Julia's. – **Erin Hagar**

Thank you, Michael, for being there through everything. I could not have done this book without the immeasurable support and encouragement of Violet Lemay. And thank you to Darrell and Kristen for being patrons of the arts. – **Joanna Gorham**